CW00432514

Hospitality Department
Instruction Booklet

The How and Why of Hospitality

"And the multitude of them that believed were of one heart and of one soul: . . . they had all things common" (Acts 4:32)

Created by Carlton L. Coon Sr.

Acknowledgements

Very little of significance is accomplished by one man acting alone. The ideas contained in this booklet are not mine. They are the result of a task force having brain-stormed for several sessions. Much of the writing and the plan itself is from them as well. My thanks to them for a simple plan of action that will help us advance the gospel.

Larry Bagley

David Smith

Tanya Smith

Tammy Foster

Diane Rose

Lee Suttles

Debbie Suttles

Bob Burk

Jeri Burk

Carmen Butler

HOSPITALITY DEPARTMENT INSTRUCTION BOOKLET. Copyright©1994, 2012 by Carlton L. Coon Sr. All rights reserved. Printed in USA. No part of this book may be used or reproduced in any manner without written permission.

Copyright 2017 – second edition, Carlton L. Coon Sr.

ISBN 10: 1545149224

ISBN 13 is 9781545149225;

Dear Partner in Evangelism,

Greetings!

The New Testament speaks of those who are "given to hospitality." The ability to create a sense of welcome for those who visit is vital. Long before a pastor or guest evangelist reads their text, the average visitor has already decided whether or not to return.

The process of creating a sense of welcome is intentional and requires consistent work. Some of the most professional church environments can be as forbidding as a hospital waiting room.

The information here comes from years of local church effort. Things can be done and taught to equip an entire church body to be more welcoming to new people. This manual is an invitation to get intentionally involved in helping reach those who will attend your church.

Your investment of time, mental energy, and spiritual desire is needed and appreciated. The long term benefits will not be measured only by what happens as your church grows. Heaven will be the real showcase.

In Christian Service,

Carlton L. Coon, Sr.

Table of Contents

Acknowledgements 2

Introduction 5

Outline for the Hospitality Department 6

Resources and Solutions 8

Job Description – Director of Hospitality 13

Job Description – Doorkeeper 15

Job Description – Greeter 17

Job Description – Guide 19

Job Description – Host/Hostess 21

Job Description – Parking Lot Attendant 23

Job Description – Usher 25

Appendix A: Apostolic Church Diagnostics Hospitality Assessment 27

Appendix B: Apostolic Church Hospitality Taskforce Resource 29

Appendix C: Guest Card 34

Appendix D: Guest Roster 35

Ordering Information 36

Introduction

It has often been said that one never gets a second chance to make a first impression. This is especially true at church.

The term "hospitality" is used four times in the New Testament. Bishops were to be "given to hospitality" (I Timothy 3:2), but all of those addressed in Romans are also encouraged to be "given to hospitality" (Romans 12:13).

There are several principles that will create a warm and hospitable atmosphere for all who visit.

- Each newcomer should be made to feel special, but not spotlighted.
- Each newcomer should meet several members of the church family.
- The "rights" of a single individual should never be allowed to infringe on the comfort or enjoyment of the entire group (i.e. a parent with a crying child should excuse him/herself to go to the nursery or the behavior of an unruly teenager should be addressed).

In pursuit of creating a ministry of hospitality, a focus group was called together to gain several perspectives on needs in this area. Additionally, several other expert resources were used. The plan of action and training material in this book are a result of the information gathered. From this point on, we start the process of implementation.

As I have said before, we have no "sacred cows the ministry of hospitality. Creating a warm, hospitable atmosphere is more important than how it's done.

At the end of this booklet in Appendices A and B, you will find the Apostolic Church Diagnostics Hospitality Assessment and Taskforce resource. The instrument will help you in assessing the effectiveness of your local assembly's hospitality in regards to guest care and the taskforce resource will provide you with the tools you need to begin. Prayerfully complete the assessment instrument and then start the work of creating an atmosphere where everyone feels welcome in your church!

Outline for the Hospitality Department

I. When weather is inclement, a parking lot attendant will meet each person who attends or visits this assembly.

The parking lot attendant will escort guests, ladies, those with infants, and elders from their car to the front door. The reason behind this is to provide an immediate positive sense of welcome for all who visit. Using an umbrella during bad weather will also help establish an attitude of care and concern.

II. Doorkeepers with a ready smile dressed in an usher's coat or some other identifying name tag, etc. will be at the front door to greet all who enter.

The doorkeeper provides a second smiling contact before a person enters the church. Doorkeepers will provide bulletins to everyone who enters and tithing or offering envelopes to those who request them.

III. A host/hostess at the information booth will provide the newcomer with a welcome packet and make their acquaintance.

The information area should be near the entryway. The host/hostess will have the guest complete a guest information card (Appendix C) and will put his/her name on the guest roster (Appendix D).

If the newcomer has a child who needs guidance to a classroom, guides are there to escort the child (and his/her parents, if they so choose) to the child's classroom. If a parent seems to have reservations about this, the guide should invite the parent to visit the classroom. If the guest has an infant, the guide will show the guest to the nursery and introduce the nursery staff. Present the nursery as an option, not a requirement.

IV. Standing just inside the auditorium will be ushers who will offer to seat guests.

Ushers should introduce themselves to anyone he/she does not know. Ask the guest if he/she has a seating preference. The usher provides a note of care when he/she asks, "May I help you in finding a seat?" If the guest accepts the offer of help, the usher should then ask, "Do you have friends who are part of our church?" If the guest does, the usher asks, "Would you like me to seat you near them?"

After seating the guest, the usher should restate his/her name and say, "If you need anything, please let me know."

V. After the newcomers are seated, three designated greeters will stop by to welcome each family.

Greeters will not be designated by any badge, coat, etc. They are to work toward holding a conversation with each guest. Greeters should be trained to lead the conversation, allowing the newcomers to talk about themselves.

		Take care not to bombard the guests with greetings and questions all at once. Space out your introductions at comfortable intervals.
VI.	During the first fifteen minutes of service, doorkeepers and hosts/hostesses should remain at their stations.	Near the end of the worship service, the host/hostess gives the guest roster to an usher to take to the pastor. Completed guest information cards are given to the director of Follow-Up Visitation.
		It is essential that you not miss a single person who visits so ushers and greeters should keep an eye open for latecomers.
VII.	Ushers have several vital roles to fill throughout the service.	During the service, ushers receive the offering, assist latecomers in finding seats, and assist in keeping order throughout the building.
		Ushers are key to having a ministry of hospitality. Their kindness sets the tone of the guest's visit, even before he/she meets the pastor.
		After the offering is received, ushers should do an exterior walk-around to ensure security in the parking lot and surrounding areas.
		Ushers should also be attentive to the pastor's needs at all times before, during, and immediately after service.
VIII.	At the close of service, doorkeepers, hosts, and parking lot attendants should be back at their posts.	Hosts should procure guest information from those who arrived late. Parking lot attendants should provide assistance as needed.
		The last thing a guest should hear is, "We are glad you came. Please come again (next service day and time)."
		Ushers and doorkeepers must lead in keeping traffic flowing and the hallways clear from unattended children.
IX.	Hospitality personnel are scheduled on a monthly basis.	All hosts, ushers, greeters, and parking lot attendants are reminded by telephone or text the day before they are to serve. This provides a smooth organizational flow.

Resources and Solutions

The following section offers resources and solutions for creating a hospitable atmosphere in the local assembly.

I. Hospitality Facility Maintenance

    A. Check restrooms before services to be certain they are clean and stocked. The appearance and cleanliness of the ladies restroom is one of the defining moments for the lady visiting for the first time.

    B. Greeters should do a walk through before going to the assigned doors. If restrooms are in need of attention, greeters should know where the restocking materials are kept.

    C. Ushers should walk through the auditorium before services to make sure song books are put away, any trash on or under seats is removed, and the altar and platform areas are cleared of clutter. This process should not be considered a part of the normal facilities cleaning and maintenance program.

II. Guest Parking

    A. The facility must have adequate parking available for both church members and guests. Research suggests that in most parts of North America there will be four cars for every seven people in attendance (a ratio of 1.75 people for each car). As a general rule, an inadequate parking area means people actually drive away from the church. If the church seats 600, but it only has 150 parking spaces available, the church's attendance is not likely to exceed 265 until additional parking becomes available.

    B. Convert about 5-7% (a minimum of two spaces) of the parking spaces closest to the entrance doors as reserved for guests. If this is a "do it yourself" project, pavement marking paints are available at most home improvement warehouse (Lowe's, Home Depot, etc.) or hardware stores.

    C. Paint the lines for guest parking a different color than the church parking. Install "Guest Parking" signs. Guests are frequently among the last to arrive on the parking lot so they should have a convenient place to park. This communicates to the church family that guests are expected and important.

III. Facilities Layout and Signage

    A. Mark the entry to the parking area clearly as an entrance.

    B. If several entry doors are visible from the parking area, one door should be clearly marked as the main entryway to the auditorium.

C. All secondary buildings and entry-ways should be clearly marked as to their purpose.

D. All internal areas of potential need (nursery, bathrooms, water fountain, etc.) should be clearly marked. Those who have attended a church for a period of time become knowledgeable about the facility. We assume everyone else has the same knowledge. When it comes to providing hospitality to newcomers do not assume anything. You cannot over-communicate. Eliminate the need for a guest to ask where the nearest restroom is located.

For smaller churches and home missionaries consider following:

External Signage: Using a pencil, ruler, and paper make a rough layout of your buildings, driveways, exits, and all other important areas. Ask the following questions:
- Is there appropriate signage?
- Is it large enough for a person in a car to read it?
- Is additional signage needed?

If so, signs can be purchased locally or nationally through a website. Start with http://www.whitepages.com in the business category. Type "signs" and your zip code and a local list will be provided. You can also contact national providers like http://www.fastsigns.com/.

Internal Signage: Using a pencil, ruler, and paper make a rough layout of your buildings with restrooms, nursery, water fountains, fellowship hall, and other important areas labeled. Once you have identified the places where a first time guest may wish to visit, decide if you can make your own signs with programs like Microsoft Word or Publisher. If funds allow, you may wish to contract this to someone locally, or use a national provider like http://www.fastsigns.com to create long-term, professional looking signs.

IV. Guest Care

A. Someone should be assigned to greet each guest either on the parking lot or at the main entryway. The first impression of a church does not come from the pastor or music. It comes from the hospitality (or lack thereof) from the parking lot to the pew. People who can smile and provide a positive welcome make a huge impact.

B. An information desk/welcome center that should be available and clearly labeled as such.

C. The information desk/welcome center should have *current* newsletters and other information on church life. Items that answer questions (because every guest comes with questions), like a FAQ sheet for different areas of ministry, are helpful. A church newsletter/bulletin should be available so guests will have something that offers a basic outline of a Pentecostal service (with biblical references), a public church calendar, etc. The Information Desk/Welcome Center is not the place to put strong doctrinal tracts that would be better explained in a one-on-one Bible Study.

D. Ensure there is a workable procedure for getting the names and addresses of each guest. Guest information cards that are completed at the information/welcome table have proven the most effective way to glean the names and addresses of guests. A good packet of materials for the guest to take home is also helpful.

The guest's address form should be copied 3 times:
➤ One copy stays in the Information Desk/Welcome Center
➤ The second copy the head usher gives to the service director (pastor, assistant pastor, etc)
➤ The third copy goes to the proper person, perhaps a secretary or church growth secretary.

If the technology is available contact information can be put in a computer that is then made available to the appropriate staff.

E. There must be designated greeters, besides ushers, who are trained to help guests.

F. Welcome guests early in the service. This is a great practice because after this point the guests can relax and enjoy the service.

G. Give copies of the Guest Information Card to the head usher approximately halfway through the worship service. Within 30 minutes of a service having started, the guest can be greeted by name.

H. Guests who come in later can be mentioned at the end of the service if it is appropriate.

I. Create an awkward-free guest welcome. As a rule, guests do not like to be asked to stand or otherwise put in an awkward situation. One way to make them feel welcome is to read the list of names of the guests, then have the church greet each other and the guests while music is being played. Making guests feel welcomed without embarrassing them is important. Drawing them into participating in the service, through the singing and designated times for small group prayer, is vital in helping them feel at home.

J. Ushers should try to seat the guests about mid-way in the center of the auditorium on the outer edges so the guest is not climbing over church members. Pastor, you will have to teach your church about making room for guests to sit. Ushers must understand the importance of introducing guests to a church member who is seated close by.

K. Lighting and color can make a guests feel welcome or create an environment of suppression. The church should always work toward creating a light welcoming atmosphere.

L. Music should be all inclusive. Praise is not restricted to church going people. David said, "Let everything that hath breath praise the LORD. Praise ye the LORD" (Psalms 150:6).

If a guest begins to praise the Lord as the church does there is no limit to what the Holy Ghost can accomplish. We can encourage their participation by:

➤ Having anointed music. Anointing is always a product of preparation; therefore for music to be anointed it must be prepared and prayed over. A list of songs that are prepared (along with keys, parts, and words) and available for use should be on hand.

➤ Salt your newer worship songs with old hymns. *Amazing Grace* and *The Old Rugged Cross* are familiar sounds to almost any guest. Changing the beat/melody to modernize hymns is an option, but the familiar lyrics are very important.

➤ If your budget will allow, use a projector to make the lyrics available to all. If you are in a home missions or small church setting, a low-cost overhead projector may be all you need. The following two websites can give you information about projection equipment. http://www.churchmultimedia.com/how_to_buy.php and http://projector.lifetips.com/cat/59703/church-projectors

M. An engaging church family wins new people. People are not looking for a friendly church; they are looking for a friend. Saints are light and salt to the world. People can be lead to become individually engaged by the example of church leadership (beginning with the pastor and his family), the training of department heads, and the encouragement of laity. Suggested training materials include:

- How to Win Friends and Influence People by Dale Carnegie
- How To Be A People Person - John Maxwell
- Interpersonal Relationship Skills For Ministers - Jeanine Cannon Bozeman
- 25 Ways to Win with People - John Maxwell

N. Your best resources are:

1. A heart for knowledge (Proverbs 18:15).

2. A pastor or administrator who has been successful in a hospitality program (Proverbs 27:17, Proverbs 11:14).

3. Prayer for wisdom (James 1:5, Proverbs 25:11).

4. Leadership of the spirit (Luke 12:12, John 14:26).

V. Nursery

A. Have a fully staffed nursery with trained personnel available. Training should include communication with parents, providing CPR for children, registering and releasing children to authorized personnel, changing diapers, and classroom management.

B. If possible children should be segregated according to age.

C. Provide a way for a parent to check on his/her child without being disruptive to the entire nursery.

D. The nursery staff must have regularly scheduled meetings and training sessions educating them on how to handle problems and concerns. An effective nursery ministry is one of the most challenging but valuable efforts in which a church can engage. For parents of nursery-aged children, the professionalism and care provided in a nursery is one of the deciding factors on whether that family returns for a second visit. There is a wealth of information online regarding operating an effective nursery. Some have materials for sale; others provide free resources to get you headed in the right direction. A Google search of "church nursery" will lead to many websites. One site to consider is Churchnursery.com.

At the very least there should be a sign in/out sheet for parents when they leave/pick-up their children. Anyone other than the parents who is allowed to pick up a child should be pre-registered with the staff.

It is better to serve a specific need well than to attempt to serve many needs and do it poorly. Consider one nursery for younger toddlers rather than to have newborns through older toddlers all in one room together. An older toddler can hurt an infant without meaning too. If the church has the staffing available, consider a three–level nursery model: Infants, crawling toddlers, walking toddlers.

In this age of litigation, it is imperative to be proactive in protecting the local church and her members. Keeping attendance records is vital. Also, video cameras in two corners of each nursery, connected to a long-term recorder, provide a record if a member of the nursery staff is accused of misconduct. Monitors in the church foyer and just outside the nursery allowed any parent to see what was happening in the nursery at any given moment.

Job Description – Director of Hospitality

I. SUMMARY OF AUTHORITY AND RESPONSIBILITY:

To prepare and schedule each month of ushers, hosts, doorkeepers, designated greeters, and parking lot attendants for every church service.

II. DUTIES INCLUDE:

A. Ensuring that this ministry is administered in a manner that will maintain order and consistency as well as bring courtesy, and hospitality to this assembly. The hospitality positions are vital in that they make the first impression upon guests. By being warm and friendly to all who come to the house of God, they foster an atmosphere through which God can move.

B. Providing a monthly schedule to all hospitality staff so they are aware of when and where they are scheduled to serve.

C. Ensuring each service will be staffed with at least one doorkeeper per entrance, one host per hosting desk, and two ushers. Parking lot attendants will be assigned during inclement weather.

D. Providing all staff with guidelines concerning attire and conduct, and ensuring the guidelines are followed.

E. Ensuring all hospitality personnel are present for prayer 40 minutes prior to service and are at their assigned posts at least 20 minutes prior to service.

F. Assigning a suitable replacement when a member of the hospitality staff is unable to fulfill his/her duties or are non-compliant with staff guidelines.

G. Informing the appropriate person of any absentees from the scheduled hospitality staff.

H. Providing adequate supplies for the hosting desk (writing utensils, guest cards, guest rosters, etc.).

I. Ensuring the host has compiled the guests' information and has filled out the guest roster to be given to an usher before the end of worship service.

J. Ensuring an usher has given the completed guest roster to the pastor and all guest cards have been given to the director of Follow-up Visitation.

III. ACCOUNTABLE TO:
- Pastor
- Aide of pastor's choosing

IV. PRINCIPAL CONSTITUENTS:
- Pastor
- Aide of pastor's choosing
- Hospitality ministry team

- Guests

V. EVALUATION:

The pastor and director will meet quarterly and jointly assess any changes that may be needed in the job description as well as additional personnel that may be required.

I HAVE READ THE JOB DESCRIPTION AND UNDERSTAND ITS RESPONSIBILITIES AND THE THINGS FOR WHICH I AM ACCOUNTABLE. I AM COMMITTED TO SERVING IN THIS CAPACITY TO THE BEST OF MY ABILITY.

_____

DIRECTOR OF HOSPITALITY SIGNATURE

I COMMIT MYSELF TO OFFERING THE SUPPORT AND GUIDANCE NECESSARY FOR YOU TO DO THE JOB TO WHICH YOU HAVE COMMITTED YOURSELF. I HAVE UTMOST CONFIDENCE IN YOUR ABILITY TO DO THE TASK WHICH HAS BEEN DELEGATED TO YOU.

_____

PASTOR SIGNATURE

Job Description – Doorkeeper

I. SUMMARY OF RESPONSIBILITY:

The doorkeeper greets all arriving church members and guests and minds the doors at the entrance door(s) of the church building. The doorkeeper is a very open and highly visible position. The first few steps of the "first impression" begins at this station. This can be the first positive step toward someone turning their life over to the Lord.

II. DUTIES INCLUDE:

A. Arriving for pre-service prayer 40 minutes prior to church time.

B. Being situated at your assigned area 20 minutes prior to church time.

C. Following the guidelines concerning attire and conduct as befitting a doorkeeper.

D. Opening and holding the entrance door for everyone (no exceptions).

E. Greeting everyone with a genuine smile, a reasonably firm handshake, and a cheerful and enthusiastic verbal greeting that is welcoming in nature. Refrain from holding conversations whenever possible. Direct any questions or inquiries requiring more than a few seconds to answer to the hostess or an usher, especially if others are approaching the door.

F. Keeping the foot traffic through the entrance doors as continuous and smooth as possible.

G. Using discretion when leaving your post and ensure that someone can replace you for the time you are gone. Return to your post as soon as possible.

H. Never express criticism toward anyone even if playful or teasing in nature. This can be misunderstood when overheard by a guest.

I. Remaining at your post until 10 minutes after the start of service.

J. Attending all meetings and training sessions as they are called by the pastor, director of hospitality, or administrative aide.

K. Being an example in prayer, praise, church attendance, and bringing guests to church. You are in a position of leadership. God honors faithfulness.

III. ACCOUNTABLE TO:

- Director of Hospitality
- Aide of pastor's choosing

IV. PRINCIPAL CONSTITUENTS:

- Pastor
- Aide of pastor's choosing
- Church members
- Director of hospitality

- Guests

V. EVALUATION:
Quarterly as a team and individually with the director of hospitality as the need arises for training or instruction.

I HAVE READ THE JOB DESCRIPTION AND UNDERSTAND ITS RESPONSIBILITIES AND THE THINGS FOR WHICH I AM ACCOUNTABLE. I AM COMMITTED TO SERVING IN THIS CAPACITY TO THE BEST OF MY ABILITY.

_____
DOORKEEPER SIGNATURE

I COMMIT MYSELF TO OFFERING THE SUPPORT AND GUIDANCE NECESSARY FOR YOU TO DO THE JOB TO WHICH YOU HAVE COMMITTED YOURSELF. I HAVE UTMOST CONFIDENCE IN YOUR ABILITY TO DO THE TASK WHICH HAS BEEN DELEGATED TO YOU.

_____
DIRECTOR OF HOSPITALITY SIGNATURE

I AM AWARE OF, COMMITTED TO, AND SUPPORTIVE OF THIS APPOINTMENT. I WILL ASSIST IN PROVIDING TRAINING AS NEEDED.

_____
PASTOR SIGNATURE

Job Description – Greeter

I. <u>SUMMARY OF RESPONSIBILITY:</u>

Greeters are designated individuals who introduce themselves and converse with all guests once the guests have entered the sanctuary. Greeters are those with a warm welcome and smile that will leave a lasting impression on guests and let them know we are interested in them by holding a brief conversation. The greeter's approach will be casual and congenial.

II. <u>DUTIES INCLUDE:</u>

A. Arriving for pre-service prayer 40 minutes prior to church time.

B. Being situated at your assigned area 20 minutes prior to church time.

C. Following the guidelines concerning attire and conduct as befitting a greeter.

D. Placing yourself in a position within the sanctuary so as to observe all guests as they enter.

   1. In a casual and unhurried manner, approach guests after they are seated.

   2. Give them a warm welcome, a smile, and a handshake. Strike up a casual conversation. Training will be provided on guiding a conversation.

   3. After a brief conversation, move on so other greeters can meet the guests. Coordinate with other assigned greeters so the guests are not asked the same questions by each greeter.

   4. Greeters will not be designated with name tags or badges as we wish to leave the impression that people at this assembly do not have to be tasked with being friendly to guests.

E. Continuing to greet guests and church members until service begins. If you see you have missed a guest, attempt to make contact with them when the whole-congregation meet and greet begins.

F. After service try to invite as many guests as possible to return. Be sure to include the next date and time the church family meets.

G. If possible additional conversation with the guest would be in order after service.

H. Attending training sessions as they are called for by the pastor, aide of pastor's choosing, or director of hospitality.

I. Being an example in prayer, praise, church attendance, and bringing guests to church. You are in a position of leadership. God honors faithfulness.

III. <u>ACCOUNTABLE TO:</u>

- Director of Hospitality
- Aide of pastor's choosing

IV. <u>PRINCIPAL CONSTITUENTS:</u>
- Pastor
- Aide of pastor's choosing
- Church members
- Director of hospitality
- Guests

V. <u>EVALUATION:</u>
Quarterly as a team and individually with the director of hospitality as the need arises for training or instruction.

I HAVE READ THE JOB DESCRIPTION AND UNDERSTAND ITS RESPONSIBILITIES AND THE THINGS FOR WHICH I AM ACCOUNTABLE. I AM COMMITTED TO SERVING IN THIS CAPACITY TO THE BEST OF MY ABILITY.

_____
GREETER SIGNATURE

I COMMIT MYSELF TO OFFERING THE SUPPORT AND GUIDANCE NECESSARY FOR YOU TO DO THE JOB TO WHICH YOU HAVE COMMITTED YOURSELF. I HAVE UTMOST CONFIDENCE IN YOUR ABILITY TO DO THE TASK WHICH HAS BEEN DELEGATED TO YOU.

_____
DIRECTOR OF HOSPITALITY SIGNATURE

I AM AWARE OF, COMMITTED TO, AND SUPPORTIVE OF THIS APPOINTMENT. I WILL ASSIST IN PROVIDING TRAINING AS NEEDED.

_____
PASTOR SIGNATURE

Job Description – Guide

J. <u>SUMMARY OF RESPONSIBILITY:</u>

A guide will sometimes have several responsibilities, all of which require friendliness and a pleasant smile. Guides will see to it that guests' children are taken to their respective classrooms. If a parent desires to see the classroom, or any other part of the church facility, your responsibility is to take them. This prevents guests from becoming confused concerning locations within the building. This position is filled only on Sunday mornings.

II. <u>DUTIES INCLUDE:</u>

A. Arriving for pre-service prayer 40 minutes prior to church time.

B. Being situated at your assigned area 20 minutes prior to church time.

C. Following the guidelines concerning attire and conduct as befitting a guide.

D. Placing yourself in the foyer near the information desk. This enables you to be immediately available to lead guests and their children to their respective classes.

E. Escorting children to their classrooms and introducing the child by name to the teacher.

F. Never remaining away from the information desk longer than 2-3 minutes.

G. Being open and willing to follow any other directions or requests by the pastor or director of hospitality. Sometimes out of the ordinary situations occur and your assistance may be needed.

H. Remaining in the foyer until 15 minutes after the service begins on Sunday mornings and then return to your own classroom area.

I. Attending training sessions as they are called for by the pastor, aide of pastor's choosing, or director of hospitality.

J. Being an example in prayer, praise, church attendance, and bringing guests to church. You are in a position of leadership. God honors faithfulness.

K. <u>ACCOUNTABLE TO:</u>
- Director of Hospitality
- Aide of pastor's choosing

L. <u>PRINCIPAL CONSTITUENTS:</u>
- Pastor
- Aide of pastor's choosing
- Church members
- Director of hospitality
- Guests

M. EVALUATION:
Quarterly as a team and individually with the director of hospitality as the need arises for training or instruction.

I HAVE READ THE JOB DESCRIPTION AND UNDERSTAND ITS RESPONSIBILITIES AND THE THINGS FOR WHICH I AM ACCOUNTABLE. I AM COMMITTED TO SERVING IN THIS CAPACITY TO THE BEST OF MY ABILITY.

_____
GUIDE SIGNATURE

I COMMIT MYSELF TO OFFERING THE SUPPORT AND GUIDANCE NECESSARY FOR YOU TO DO THE JOB TO WHICH YOU HAVE COMMITTED YOURSELF. I HAVE UTMOST CONFIDENCE IN YOUR ABILITY TO DO THE TASK WHICH HAS BEEN DELEGATED TO YOU.

_____
DIRECTOR OF HOSPITALITY SIGNATURE

I AM AWARE OF, COMMITTED TO, AND SUPPORTIVE OF THIS APPOINTMENT. I WILL ASSIST IN PROVIDING TRAINING AS NEEDED.

_____
PASTOR SIGNATURE

Job Description – Host/Hostess

I. <u>SUMMARY OF RESPONSIBILITY:</u>

The hosting team provides a personal welcome to each guest to this assembly. The host/hostess will also assist the guest in filling out the information card and connecting them with a guide as needed.

III. <u>DUTIES INCLUDE:</u>

A. Arriving for pre-service prayer 40 minutes prior to church time.

B. Being situated at your assigned area 20 minutes prior to church time.

C. Following the guidelines concerning attire and conduct as befitting a host/hostess.

D. Assisting guests in filling out the guest information card.

E. Preparing the guest roster seating chart for the pastor's use. Include the name of infrequent attendees even if they call this assembly home. This will help the pastor recognize their attendance.

F. Remaining at the hosting desk until 10 minutes after the service begins to provide information to late arrivals.

G. Providing an usher the completed guest roster sheet 15 minutes after service begins.

H. Greeting (after service) all guests who arrived after the hosting desk was vacated for service. Assist them in filling out a guest information card.

I. Providing all completed guest information cards to the director of follow-up visitation.

J. Attending training sessions as they are called for by the pastor, aide of pastor's choosing, or director of hospitality.

K. Being an example in prayer, praise, church attendance, and bringing guests to church. You are in a position of leadership. God honors faithfulness.

L. <u>ACCOUNTABLE TO:</u>
- Director of Hospitality
- Aide of pastor's choosing

M. <u>PRINCIPAL CONSTITUENTS:</u>
- Pastor
- Aide of pastor's choosing
- Church members
- Director of hospitality
- Guests

N. <u>EVALUATION:</u>

Quarterly as a team and individually with the director of hospitality as the need arises for training or instruction.

I HAVE READ THE JOB DESCRIPTION AND UNDERSTAND ITS RESPONSIBILITIES AND THE THINGS FOR WHICH I AM ACCOUNTABLE. I AM COMMITTED TO SERVING IN THIS CAPACITY TO THE BEST OF MY ABILITY.

_____
HOSTING TEAM MEMBER SIGNATURE

I COMMIT MYSELF TO OFFERING THE SUPPORT AND GUIDANCE NECESSARY FOR YOU TO DO THE JOB TO WHICH YOU HAVE COMMITTED YOURSELF. I HAVE UTMOST CONFIDENCE IN YOUR ABILITY TO DO THE TASK WHICH HAS BEEN DELEGATED TO YOU.

_____
DIRECTOR OF HOSPITALITY SIGNATURE

I AM AWARE OF, COMMITTED TO, AND SUPPORTIVE OF THIS APPOINTMENT. I WILL ASSIST IN PROVIDING TRAINING AS NEEDED.

_____
PASTOR SIGNATURE

Job Description – Parking Lot Attendant

I. <u>SUMMARY OF RESPONSIBILITY:</u>

The parking lot attendant provides assistance in maintaining order and safety in the parking areas of the church. A parking lot attendant is generally the first representative of the church a guest sees.

II. <u>DUTIES INCLUDE:</u>

A. Arriving for pre-service prayer 40 minutes prior to church time.

B. Being situated at your assigned area 20 minutes prior to church time.

C. Following the guidelines concerning attire and conduct as befitting a parking lot attendant.

D. Carrying an umbrella in times of inclement weather.

E. Assisting guests and regular church members in any way possible. Elders often require assistance in the parking areas (especially over uneven surfaces) as well as climbing steps. Parents frequently require assistance in carrying items necessary for caring for very young children.

F. Directing drivers to supplemental parking areas if lot is full.

G. Remaining at your post until 15 minutes after the service begins. At the approximate halfway mark of the service, make a security walk through the parking lot. If any issues (even suspected ones) arise, notify the director of hospitality or an usher immediately.

H. Attending training sessions as they are called for by the pastor, aide of pastor's choosing, or director of hospitality.

I. Being an example in prayer, praise, church attendance, and bringing guests to church. You are in a position of leadership. God honors faithfulness.

J. <u>ACCOUNTABLE TO:</u>
   - Director of Hospitality
   - Aide of pastor's choosing

K. <u>PRINCIPAL CONSTITUENTS:</u>
   - Pastor
   - Aide of pastor's choosing
   - Church members
   - Director of hospitality
   - Guests

L. <u>EVALUATION:</u>

Quarterly as a team and individually with the director of hospitality as the need arises for training or instruction.

I HAVE READ THE JOB DESCRIPTION AND UNDERSTAND ITS RESPONSIBILITIES AND THE THINGS FOR WHICH I AM ACCOUNTABLE. I AM COMMITTED TO SERVING IN THIS CAPACITY TO THE BEST OF MY ABILITY.

_____
PARKING LOT ATTENDANT SIGNATURE

I COMMIT MYSELF TO OFFERING THE SUPPORT AND GUIDANCE NECESSARY FOR YOU TO DO THE JOB TO WHICH YOU HAVE COMMITTED YOURSELF. I HAVE UTMOST CONFIDENCE IN YOUR ABILITY TO DO THE TASK WHICH HAS BEEN DELEGATED TO YOU.

_____
DIRECTOR OF HOSPITALITY SIGNATURE

I AM AWARE OF, COMMITTED TO, AND SUPPORTIVE OF THIS APPOINTMENT. I WILL ASSIST IN PROVIDING TRAINING AS NEEDED.

_____
PASTOR SIGNATURE

Job Description – Usher

I. <u>SUMMARY OF RESPONSIBILITY:</u>

The ushers of this assembly are tasked with establishing a friendly, safe, and disciplined environment in which both guests and church members can feel comfortable. It is the essential ministry of servanthood to those who are at church.

II. <u>DUTIES INCLUDE:</u>

A. Arriving for pre-service prayer 40 minutes prior to church time.

B. Being situated at your assigned area inside the church auditorium doors 20 minutes prior to church time.

C. Following the guidelines concerning attire and conduct as befitting an usher.

D. Greeting all those who enter the sanctuary.

E. Offering to help guests find a seat.

F. Handing out bulletins and tithing/offering envelopes as needed.

G. Assisting in procuring and setting up any special equipment needed for the service.

H. Remaining near the back door to assist those who arrive late with finding a seat.

I. Maintaining order in both the auditorium and the hallway before, during, and after service. Children, teens, intoxicated guests, etc., should be corrected as kindly as possible. However, the rights of one shall never infringe on the blessings of many.

J. Assisting parents with fussy babies/toddlers in finding the nursery.

K. Receiving the offering and delivering it to the appropriate individual or place.

L. Counting cash and reporting the amount to the pastor if he has requested it.

M. Requesting those who have left the service and wish to return during the preaching to sit near the back when possible.

N. Handling emergency situations with maturity and calmness.

O. Assisting the pastor as needed.

P. Providing the pastor the completed guest roster at the end of worship service.

Q. Assisting in securing the building after services: checking all AC/heating units, ensuring appropriate doors are locked, and turning off the lights.

R. Attending training sessions as they are called for by the pastor, aide of pastor's choosing, or director of hospitality.

S. Being an example in prayer, praise, church attendance, and bringing guests to church. You are in a position of leadership. God honors faithfulness.

T. <u>ACCOUNTABLE TO:</u>
- Pastor
- Director of Hospitality
- Aide of pastor's choosing

U. <u>PRINCIPAL CONSTITUENTS:</u>
- Pastor
- Aide of pastor's choosing
- Church members
- Director of hospitality
- Guests

V. <u>EVALUATION:</u>
Quarterly as a team and individually with the director of hospitality as the need arises for training or instruction.

I HAVE READ THE JOB DESCRIPTION AND UNDERSTAND ITS RESPONSIBILITIES AND THE THINGS FOR WHICH I AM ACCOUNTABLE. I AM COMMITTED TO SERVING IN THIS CAPACITY TO THE BEST OF MY ABILITY.

_____
USHER SIGNATURE

I COMMIT MYSELF TO OFFERING THE SUPPORT AND GUIDANCE NECESSARY FOR YOU TO DO THE JOB TO WHICH YOU HAVE COMMITTED YOURSELF. I HAVE UTMOST CONFIDENCE IN YOUR ABILITY TO DO THE TASK WHICH HAS BEEN DELEGATED TO YOU.

_____
DIRECTOR OF HOSPITALITY SIGNATURE

I AM AWARE OF, COMMITTED TO, AND SUPPORTIVE OF THIS APPOINTMENT. I WILL ASSIST IN PROVIDING TRAINING AS NEEDED.

_____
PASTOR SIGNATURE

Appendix A: Apostolic Church Diagnostics Hospitality Assessment

In order to assess the effectiveness of this church's hospitality in regards to guest care, provide the best answer to the following questions. Every area is important. With each question you will find helpful information that will help you improve in the needed area. The statistics and solutions being provided are not relevant for every church. Urban churches where attendees travel by bus or subway have a different dynamic.

I. Guest Parking

    A. Our auditorium can seat _____ .

    B. We have _____ on-site parking spaces available at this facility.

    C. There are _____ parking spaces set aside for guests.

II. Facilities Layout and Signage (circle one)

    A. Is the entry to the parking area clearly marked as an entrance?   Y/N

    B. If several entry doors are visible from the parking area, is one door clearly marked as the main entryway to the auditorium?   Y/N

    C. Are all secondary buildings and entry-ways clearly marked as to their purpose?   Y/N

    D. Are all internal areas of potential need (nursery, bathrooms, water fountain, etc.) clearly marked?   Y/N

    Those who have attended a church for a period of time become knowledgeable about

III. Welcoming Guests

    A. Is someone assigned to greet each guest either on the parking lot or at the main entryway?   Y/N

    B. Is there an information/welcome table that is clearly labeled as such?   Y/N

    C. Does the information/welcome table have *current* newsletters and other information on church life?   Y/N

    D. Is there a workable procedure for getting the names and addresses of each guest?   Y/N

    E. Are there designated greeters, besides ushers, who are trained to help guests?   Y/N

    F. Is there a program in place to clean and maintain guest-frequented areas?   Y/N

IV. The Guest During the Service

A. Do you welcome guests early in the service?   Y/N

B. Do you welcome guest without making them stand or creating awkwardness for them?   Y/N

C. Is your music, whatever style, done well and will guests be able to participate in the singing?   Y/N

D. Is there a workable procedure for getting the names and addresses of each guest?   Y/N

E. Are there designated greeters, besides ushers, who are trained to help guests?   Y/N

F. Do your members engage guests and invite them to coffee or other social activities after the service, taking the initiative to introduce them to other church members?   Y/N

V. Nursery

A. In two sentences describe the nursery services provided by the church.

_____

_____

_____

_____

_____

B. Do trained personnel staff the nursery?   Y/N
   (Training should include communication with parents, providing CPR for children, registering and releasing children to authorized personnel, changing diapers, and classroom management.)

C. Are children segregated according to age?   Y/N

D. Is there some way for a parent to check on his/her child without being disruptive to the entire nursery?   Y/N

E. Does the nursery staff have regularly scheduled meetings and training sessions educating them on how to handle problems and concerns?   Y/N

Appendix B: Apostolic Church Hospitality Taskforce Resource

This resource will assist in preparing your church to meet the needs of the congregation and community through excellence in hospitality and guest care.

Our Mission

To create a mindset in the congregation that encourages a constant awareness of those who will visit this assembly. If churches do not have visitors they do not have growth

Our Process

Developing a research-driven presentation that will facilitate a "buy-in" by every member of this congregation.

Pastor, begin by prayerfully choosing an individual who is capable and willing to chair the taskforce committee. The first step in this journey will be for that individual to create a timeline for the entire project, beginning with research collection and interpretation and ending with a presentation of the report to the entire church body.

A hospitality taskforce working alongside the pastor and other key leaders will conduct a research project that examines this church from the perspective of a visitor. The hospitality taskforce will be divided into subgroups. Each group will then use visual media to share personal observations about their discoveries. The hospitality taskforce will endeavor to assess the total church experience as though they were first time guests to this congregation. Each subgroup will develop a list of areas that need to be evaluated. The entire taskforce will find ways to improve a guest's experience for that first visit. Our goal is to turn "first timers" into "full-timers."

The first taskforce meeting should be driven by the following questions:
- What is involved in a setting where you feel you are being treated hospitably?
- What are an usher, a host/hostess, a doorkeeper, and a greeter? Define using your own words.
- How can we balance the essentials of hospitality with maintaining order and security?
- How long has it been since you visited another church as a visitor? What positive thing do you remember about the experience? What negative thing do you recall?
- Looking back, if you had the power to change the experience in a way that would have benefitted you as a visitor, what would you have done?
- How can we awaken our church to the grand opportunity that lies before us?

Hospitality Taskforce

Subgroup 1

"Our Church from the Highway"

This subgroup is tasked with observing the church from the point of view of passersby and making recommendations for improvements in the area "curb appeal."

I.   Signage
   A. What does the sign communicate about our church?
   B. What does it tell you about upcoming events?
   C. If you look at nothing but the sign, what do you think of the church?
   D. Does anything seem lacking from the sign(s)?

Making the Point: Take pictures from all angles of church sign.

II.   Landscaping
   A. What does the landscaping portray about our church facilities and the people who attend church here?
   B. When you look at the lawn and grounds, what do you imagine as being the mindset of the people who attend this church?

Making the Point: Take pictures of our church's landscape, both good and bad. Look at the places nobody but our neighbors see.

III.   Campus
   A. Does the building have a modern look?
   B. Does the physical plant need a face-lift (paint, repairs, etc.)?
   C. Does current condition communicate progress or lack of concern?
   D. Is the campus well lit at night and does it appear to be safe? As a woman, elder, or disabled individual would I be concerned about getting to my vehicle after dark?

Making the Point: Take pictures of the building at various times and from different angles. Does it appear open for business during office hours?

Recommendations

1. Please attach a list containing your recommendations for improving church appearance from all exterior viewpoints.

2. Please attach a list containing your recommendations for improving a guest's experience on the church's parking lot.

Hospitality Taskforce

Subgroup 2

"Our Church from the Vehicle to the Door"

This subgroup is tasked with experiencing the church from the point of view of the first time guest and making recommendations for improvements in this area.

   I.   Walking towards the building
        A. Which door do I enter? (Consider this from every possible parking spot).
        B. Who is that group of young men and women there on the steps?
        C. Am I dressed appropriately?
        D. How will I find the classroom for my children?
        E. Will I know anyone?
        F. Is anyone here like me?
        G. What am I doing here?
        H. How do I find the person who invited me?

   II.   Does anyone provide a warm welcome before I reach the door?

Recommendations

Please attach a list containing your recommendations for improving the guest's experience as he/she walks from the vehicle to the entrance.

Hospitality Taskforce

Subgroup 3

"Our Church at the Door"

This subgroup is tasked with experiencing the church from the point of view of the first time guest as he/she enters the door and making recommendations for improvements in this area.

I.   Walking in the door
- A. Does someone greet me? If so how?
  1. Do they act glad to see me?
  2. How do they open the door?
  3. What do they look like (appearance)?
  4. Are they what I expected?
- B. What do I see in the foyer?
  1. Is it warm and inviting or cold and withdrawn?
  2. Do I feel lost in it or is there an obvious place for me to start?

II.   Foyer Greetings
- A. Does a host/hostess greet me and introduce him/herself?
  1. Does anything mark him/her as an official representative of the church?
  2. Does he/she ask me for my name and address? How does he/she ask?
- B. What information about the church is provided to me?

Recommendations

Please attach a list containing your recommendations for improving the guest's experience at the entrance and in the foyer of the church.

Hospitality Taskforce

Subgroup 4

"Our Church Building"

This subgroup is tasked with experiencing the church from the point of view of the first time guest as he/she attempts to navigate our facilities and making recommendations for improvements in this area.

I.   From the inside
    A. Are there signs point to the restrooms?
    B. Where is the nursery? Are there signs?
        1. Does a guide introduce me to the nursery attendant?
        2. Does a nursery attendant ask if I know where I would be sitting?
        3. Does a nursery attendant ask me if there are any special needs or instructions concerning the care of my child?
        4. Is there a way for a nursery attendant to contact me in the sanctuary should the need arise?
    C. Are there classrooms?
        1. Is there a guide available to direct me and my children to the age-appropriate classrooms?
        2. Is there a designated area where I can reconnect with my children after service?
        3. Is this clearly communicated to me?

II. From the sanctuary
    A. Is the sanctuary clean and inviting?
    B. Have I been welcomed by people other than the usher and greeters?
    C. What are the sounds in the sanctuary? Is the audio level too high or too low?
    D. Is the beginning of the service planned and organized?
    E. Am I made to feel a part?
    F. How do I feel about the offering appeal?

III. Now that church is over
    A. Does anyone seek me out to converse?
    B. Am I invited to return and given service time information?
    C. Does anyone give me a chance to ask questions?

Recommendations

Please attach a list containing your recommendations for improving the guest's knowledge about the church facilities and campus.

Appendix C: Guest Card

GUEST INFORMATION CARD

Name (please print)	Date

Street Address	Phone Number

City	State/Province	Postal Code

Referred by/Guest of	Home Church

Please circle your age group: *13-18*   *19-25*   *26-35*   *36 & older*

If you brought children with you what are their ages? _____

How did you first hear about us? (Circle one)   *Friend   Advertisement   Walk-In   Other*

If you circled "Advertisement" or "Other," please describe: _____

Are you interested in receiving information about any of the following ministries? (circle all that apply)

Children   *Teen/Youth*   *Singles*   *Young Married*

Appendix D: Guest Roster

Date: _____ A.M./P.M.   Host: _____

Name:	Guest of:	1st Time Guest	Seated (row and approximate seat number)
		Y N	
_____	_____	Y N	_____
_____	_____	Y N	_____
_____	_____	Y N	_____
_____	_____	Y N	_____
_____	_____	Y N	_____
_____	_____	Y N	_____
_____	_____	Y N	_____
_____	_____	Y N	_____
_____	_____	Y N	_____
_____	_____	Y N	_____
_____	_____	Y N	_____
_____	_____	Y N	_____
_____	_____	Y N	_____

Ordering Information

Truth-Publications.com
4521 North FR 165
Springfield, MO 65803
Email orders to: carltoncoon@carltonlcoonsr.com

OR

Pentecostal Publishing House